Free Verse Editions

Edited by Jon Thompson

POEMS FROM ABOVE THE HILL

SELECTED POEMS OF ASHUR ETWEBI

Translated by Brenda Hillman and Diallah Haidar
(with the author)

Parlor Press
Anderson, South Carolina
www.parlorpress.com

Parlor Press LLC, West Lafayette, Indiana 47906

Library of Congress Cataloging-in-Publication Data

Tuwaybi, 'Ashur.
[Poems. English. Selections]
 Poems from above the hill : selected poems of Ashur Etwebi
/ translated by Brenda Hillman and Diallah Haidar (with the
author).
    p. cm. -- (Free verse editions)
 ISBN 978-1-60235-160-8 (pbk. : alk. paper) -- ISBN 978-1-
60235-161-5 (Adobe ebook)
 I. Hillman, Brenda. II. Haidar, Diallah. III. Title.
PJ7864.T92A2 2011
892.7'16--dc22
                              2010054545

Cover design by David Blakesley.
Cover Image: "The Man Coming from the East" © 2009 by
Syagci. Used by permission.

Printed on acid-free paper.

Parlor Press, LLC is an independent publisher of scholarly
and trade titles in print and multimedia formats. This book is
available in paper, cloth and Adobe eBook formats from Parlor
Press on the World Wide Web at http://www.parlorpress.com or
through online and brick-and-mortar bookstores. For submission
information or to find out about Parlor Press publications, write
to Parlor Press, 3015 Brackenberry Drive, Anderson, South
Carolina, 29621, or e-mail editor@parlorpress.com.

Contents

Translator's Note

This project came about quite by accident. I was serving as a visiting faculty member at the Iowa Writers' Workshop in fall of 2006 and attended a meeting at the International Writers' Workshop on a sunny fall afternoon. As is often the case there, the room was full of notable writers from all over the world, many of whom were expressing interest in translation. Though I do not speak Arabic, I had worked with Saadi Simawe, an Iraqi-American professor at Grinnell College, to render some versions of Iraqi poetry into English, and I mentioned this at the meeting.

Afterwards, an enthusiastic fellow bounded over to me and asked if I would work with him on his poetry. He was, he said, Dr. Ashur Etwebi from Libya, a physician-poet who was spending a few months at the International Writers' Workshop. I insisted to the gentleman that I speak not a word of Arabic and he said we must not let that deter us.

During the next two months, we met frequently at Java House, one of Iowa City's most agreeable locales, to work on his poetry. It turned out that his English is excellent — he had spent four years in London— and he brought me transliterations of a long poetic sequence he had written and published in Libya some years before, work that we ended up calling "Poems from Above the Hill." I was entirely dependent on Ashur's transliterations, of course, but we went forward because we enjoyed the process.

Ashur is a courteous and witty man, and he approached the daunting task with good cheer. As we worked on our versions, Ashur noted that he was re-casting the originals at times when we could not find an appropriate translation. This helped us relax about the project, especially about striving for fidelity to a single original text. Before he returned to Libya, we had produced poems that sounded good to both of us, and that— despite significant variations between the Arabic originals and the English translations—and they seemed to satisfy Ashur's sense of the of the originals.

Over the next few years we kept in touch, publishing the sequence in *Free Verse*. Bob Hass, Forrest Gander, CD Wright and I made a trip to Libya, where Ashur was our host for one of the most fascinating weeks of our lives—that is a story for another time. Soon after our trip, Jon Thompson, who is both an editor of *Free Verse* and an editor at Parlor Press, asked to see a larger collection of Ashur's work and we set about trying to figure out how this could be done.

In the meantime, one of Bob's students, Diallah Haidar, a Lebanese-American woman who is fluent in both Arabic and English, had fallen in love with Ashur's poetry and had done some wonderful translations, so I enlisted her help with the project. Working with Diallah has been a pleasure, and the project could not have gone more smoothly. I am also grateful for the organizing skills of Jillian Kurvers, who has been very helpful with preparation of the manuscript.

I will probably never know Ashur's poetry in the original. I am tremendously moved by his work, by the way he compactly renders experience in a hauntingly classical way. Ashur's work is rooted in the landscapes of his country, and in inventing forms in his literary traditions that will capture his engagement with his place and culture.

His poetry is intimate but grand, innovative but traditional, influenced by Modernist poetry, which he seems to have read while he was studying in England, yet populist and accessible, at least in the versions he and Diallah have presented to me. Diallah has told me repeatedly that the phrasing and syntax are often very unpredictable, risk-taking, experimenting with neologisms, inventing language— so he would be considered an experimental or innovative poet. In his work, there is often a strongly elegiac note; his irony that reminds one of Eliot, his imagistic purity that reminds one of Pound. Yet he has an intimate knowledge of his fellow creatures that brings to mind W. C.Williams. I am reminded of several other poets as well: of George Oppen, and of C. P. Cavafy. Ashur Etwebi enters the mysterious places of the land and sea through the experiences of the human beings he encounters, never engaging in sentimental homage but putting forward a powerful and delicious reverie and a poetic vision. However partial these versions are, it is to be hoped they will render some sense of the originals.

—*Brenda Hillman*

Poems from Above the Hill and Selected Work

from *Qsaed Al-Shorfa*

Poems of the Terrace

EMOTIONS

On magnetic and electrical wires I traveled
the tired and astonished distance;
I touched the gate:
beyond was a white courtyard and an intimate whisper
and figures covered with wool robes-- standing,
sitting, leaning-- were everywhere.
Advancing through the sad crowds, shielding my eyes from the sun,
I stopped and felt my heart with one hand
searching for a corner in which I hid for my beloved.
For a moment I was alone with lines of flowers and powerful water.

Exposed by the wish of the clouds,
I watched the picture evolving slowly:
these cities with their flags at the edge of the horizon,
with the souls' gardens wet to the roots,
revealed their secrets in a simple language.
These deserts at the origins of shadows gathered by hot breath
catch what I can't see,
burning me with fuel for my heated breath.
These oceans are water and salt
where the lips approach the face,
singing deeply and slowly.

Exposed by the wish of the clouds,
I gather what has fled from me
and ask permission to enter.

WHITE BIRDS IN A BLACK SPACE

He said:
you may walk into spaces of mildness and obedience
with the rebellious, the dreamers and the scared;
you know that the city has been violated,
that everything is permissible, impossible and chaotic.
You may stand under the sun,
write on its walls with the blood and wisdom
which it has hidden in a box of memory.

White birds in a black space.
Black birds in a white space.

He said:
With first light, we travel to water's edge
to escape from the siege of emotions filled with dust;
we sleep on the crowd's feeble, frightened trees,
embrace ourselves and touch the edge of ecstasy.

The ship hits hard against the water's surface;
heartlessly it destroys the dance of the waves.
On the water, two birds and a gate;
on the water, two stars and a boat;
on the water, two roses and a heart;
on the water, a dream is held up, sharp as a knife.

He said:
The men who just came from the seashore
are walking on the water
with spears in their hands
while my ship is grounded and my seashells float along.

The butterflies had stopped laughing.
They had wings made of clay
and a permanent seat in the court of fear.

He said:
You know that the sea is large
and time seeps like water between fingers until nothing remains.
You know that from the scent of lemon: a drop fell,
it penetrated the earth freshly and deeply.
You know that forests brought dates
to the lover and to the stones of joyful beaches.
The stones crashed and turned into iron flowers.
Why are you hiding rooms of modern cities,
full of futile noise, always holding young breasts
and swallowing your saliva?

The workings of the clock are suspended from a hole in the wall
and the time calmly counts commas and dots
for the new morning.
A knock on the door,
and behind the door
morning is standing.
Who wants the morning so early?

He said:
Looking for the stone in the water
and looking for the water in the stone.
It is I who am optimistic in autumn,
it is I who love the wheat woman
and is not scared of the death of silence.
In the crowd, I eat only a few words
and wink to the women passing by.
I see gazelles crying
and I see happiness killing itself in the city plaza.
I remember how the apple retreated, naked
before the moon, and how fear stopped back
and begged for forgiveness.

The alphabet on the wall
isasking the wall to turn into ash
and not to reveal the buildings' secrets.
The buildings say as they close their doors:
When the concept is clear, the police disappear.

He said:
I didn't go to the sea this evening.
I was stopped by a wailing stone.
Two stab wounds in its chest
I asked it: Who—?
It answered: You—.

The faces that fell down
from the cloud of life have passed this way,
broken, crying and shadowless.
The wrinkles and extra flesh of old winters were taken away by the
traveling ships.

He said:
I see them planting the seeds of desire,
They were kings, sitting in the cafés of silver.
I see them in the large halls and on the grand marble,
featureless.

The bird that has returned home,
it kept on with its reverie till morning,
It released the olive oil traders from jail
and poured the oil.

He said:
Many will pass through these places
but the sand remains sand.
Oh, young sand, you have become a catastrophe.
Birds of the dear country have built their nests in you;
the upper houses and lower houses flourish
and he who walked to the beating drums

wanted to reach it.
The country has besieged the kings and betrayed the prophets.

Before I understood its language,
I was naïve, I only knew what was written in the geography book
and the political report.
I was stuffed with straw.
I didn't know that sand is alive
and rain is the master and the awaited lover,
I didn't know that the sun only sits there,
that the proud cities dress when their time comes,
that the hearts flood over there
I was naïve, narrow-minded and rebellious.

He said:
You ran away from me as a lonely cloud
and when you come back
my worries will be scattered on the naked shoulder.
The candle won't melt and you are what you are;

this is the peak of fever,
this is the time for penetration
and my beloved desert country: drown yourself in perfume.

From *Asdikaak Maro Min Huna*

Your Friends Passed This Way

MARCO POLO

The structure is opened
with signs of a dead child
with closed circles
with the repetitive departure of the poem
choosing a free and untroubled body
for the beginning and end of space:

skins the color of time that has passed,
and there is danger between wood and water
and the wind rides the furtive waters;
necks float along, and eyes close on their dreams,
on bodies that have stroked the finger of a curse.

Hunters chase the thin, runaway dreams that grow

in the sweat,
        the words,
                the metal...

Too much water in the ink,
too much chirping behind the closed window
and the face is lifted by two monks
tempted by a broken wall.

To know what water can write on water:
to know the secrets of chaos tumbling in the sand,
the mystery behind words scattered by the wind...

Droplets are boundaries between serenity and what is lost.
In the town square, places, people, and flying elephants.
In the corner, a shrouded corpse and shadows of a lost father.
Candle and corpse start out together;
emptiness goes out to sea
and the father is a flutter of sighs.

This idol,
this living idol,
breathes like
      my father,
sweats like
      my father.

Humanity swells behind the archipelago,
ships return but my father doesn't
the birds return but my father doesn't;
the ghost ship appears:
what do the ghosts hide?

Fish disappear
and eyes disappear in eyes;
in Saint Luke's church, the heart is sometimes captured,
the colors remain
and the fish-girl, stone and water

In my spare time, I build my boat,
I build people in my head;
I draw my dreams
and the froth of time grows
alone under rain,
alone in the night.

Friends, wood, fire, honey,
and the splendid painting.
Bells ring,
and the town square is bustling with hollow people,
the two women,
prostitution and catharsis, meet.
The sea cries:
stay away,
stay away,
this is the end of people.

Here, madness grows like moss on the walls,
the fish will take him out to sea where the heart is going;

cruelty is the way to survive.
An evening without feet.
Four men are beating the drums,
the horse stands guard,
the bodies of the dead are pebbles on the ground
yet you search for water.
Who passed through these valleys before you?
Who shook hands with the sun by the sea?
Fear in the eyes
but the heart is dead
and betrayal stands alone.

In fever, ideas are made,
the covering over the eyes has fallen,
there is no road in the sea now,
the city is smoke,
the city is a plague.
Do you cross the river?
The snow and whiteness are vast
and the ground beneath you surrenders,
dives deep.
In the snow, the echoes of dreams don't answer.
To leave,
the sea bank is full of bodies
separated from the horses' backs.

He couldn't find a place to conquer,
he didn't leave the hunter any prey;
he washed the woman with his nakedness,
she was a cold hunger in his body.
Clear away everything nomadic and innocent.
He put his secrets onto clay,
he saw his likeness in the dream,
he complained to his mother of his defeat,
and for the first time, he was frightened and couldn't sleep.

from *Nahr Al-Mosika*

Music River

LADDERS

Here's a ladder leading to a stranger's tavern
Here's a ladder leading to a feast for the poor
Here's a ladder leading to an empty town square
Here's a ladder leading to a hanging
Here's a ladder leading to a locked forest
Here's a ladder leading to closed fragrances
Here's a ladder leading to an endless waterfall
Here's a ladder leading to a fat stick in a hole
Here's a ladder leading to a sad minaret
Here's a ladder leading to music with one tune
Here's a ladder leading to a lover's nest
Here's a ladder leading to a sad snail
Here's a ladder leading to an invisible city
Here's a ladder leading to an anxious shadow
Here's a ladder leading to a hot sigh
Here's a ladder leading to a monk's cocoon
Here's a ladder leading to a king who never leaves his throne
Here's a ladder leading to a dry creek
Here's a ladder leading to ladders leading to a ladder that leads to
ladders...

FACE

I didn't notice a face in the mud—
I was tired and angry.
The face belonged to a man—perhaps—
thin, broken down by harsh years,
the forehead narrow and bulging with a stern focus,
the bone eaten away by the dullness of moths and the worries of
dreamers,
the eyes half-closed.
Were they dreaming of pigeon collars, or were they tired of looking
in faces?

If I were to see him, would I ask him about old and forgotten
times?
About a young girl circling a familiar neighborhood?
About lost cities from past lives of those standing on the bridge?
About a short glance from the crack of a door?
About many, many words?

Maybe I could ask him about this and that.
If I hadn't overlooked his face in the mud.

SITTING

While sitting in a chair

with a shaved head and smooth cheeks, he said:
"Except for the wisdom in my heart,
serenity is my eternal garden,
and that is what I wrote on your rocks.
I was among you—
no name races ahead of me
and no shadow follows me.
You would pass by my door but would never knock.
On my windowsill,
glasses of your odor.
Your scandals are revealed;
every time I move my tongue,
it exposes me.

Here I am now, a body without breath,
tied with string to your groaning,
I watch from my window.
Perhaps one day—
just one day—
odorless fingers will knock on my door."

WHITE

Sometimes I get the feeling that the street
is white,
that the sleep of shoulders shifting heavy with medallions
is white,
that the sand hurrying to ride June winds,
is white,
the thought I have as I turn to the woman sitting behind the iron
window
is white –
even words that come as if my mother had done her prayer beads
after a hot afternoon
are white.

I don't expect
nor do I wait for an answer
because I know that white
can't speak.

LET'S STOP A WHILE

Let's stop a while
at the beginning of the road
it won't matter
at the end of the road
it won't matter
whether we hear
boiling
or dancing
it might be as cold as a frog's skin
that just came from its winter home
it could be breath sucked in
from the bottom of lungs beaten by tobacco

Can't you see
that we hang by the thread of a spider
in our fear-cave
we start to divide everything
into halves
and at the brink of our illusions
we piss on illusions
we draw a world
with a powerful memory
and set our tents
on deserts we don't own anymore

Let's stop a while
if only nobly to pretend
that the right eye
can't see
what falls
who falls
on the other side
can't you see
that the sky argues with the winter clouds
and butterflies no longer fly over our roofs

Let's stop a while
only to pour their precious wine
in eternally thirsty sands
and to be proud of our camels
that have always known
the forgotten path to hunger and emptiness

A BIRD

Bird perching on my shoulder:
you rest a little.
I carry your favorite food and my hand doesn't tire.
I clean the dust from your feathers and my other hand doesn't tire.
With my eyes, I protect you from hidden traps.
In my heart, I cradle your bed so you sleep calmly.
With my ears, I tune in to footsteps of hunters in the distance;
with my foot, I brush the scent of you from tender branches and
stems.

And my shoulder is your seat in the sky.

Bird perching on my shoulder:
did you know about this before now?

The bird says:
Life is not worth living for a bird who hates decay.

From *Sundok ADhahikat Al-Qadima*

Box of old laughs

TRIPOLI HAIKU

The bird fell down
from its new nest
The tree watches.

*

It has a golden beak,
it won't
forget its song.

*

Closed windows now.
Summer took
the last words.

*

He was dead;
the ship's captain
didn't come.

*

He opened his toothless
mouth laughing;
he didn't tell me about the price of fish.

*

When it heard
the autumn's song
fig tree got naked.

*

   With his finger he moves his tongue:
the man who wears
his scarf in the summer.

*

   Coffee cup on a table
and the man's eyes
on a cloud.

*

   Traveler's dreams –
didn't rain
this winter.

*

   Alone in the midst of trees,
in the spring,
crying throughout her old age.

*

   Her window is wide open;
the puddle
is proud of its colors.

*

Between stars
nothing
but a long glance.

*

A saddle flying in the air,
a poet
playing with words.

*

A heart as large as the sea,
a poet
taken away by a stone.

*

A poet's voice
is heard;
Now he can rest.

*

O Sea, you are calm
where
the heart boils.

*

On his bike:
wheeling& wheeling,
spreading his life.

*

In front of her jump rope,
behind her jump rope,
collecting laughter of the day.

*

Before reaching Waddan,
running between thorn trees
without looking back.

*

"The sea is furious this morning,"
said my son
pointing to a bird in the air.

*

A man holding an umbrella
with a thread
of his pink desire.

*

Windows everywhere,
windows
that have nothing.

*

Two bicycles in a graveyard,
and plates on
the soft marble.

*

White clouds
sitting in the shade,
trees with long necks.

*

They hold hands
under palm trees;
    I smile from a distance.

*

What is in the entrance
but
bones?

*

A hanging space
on
a lateral yard.

*

Coffee cups
in the shade
next to the dead man.

*

The shadow of a man
with long legs
is burning.

*

O beautiful woman,
your black and white dress
suits the forest.

*

O beautiful woman
with red lips:
where does the river run.

*

A single drop of water,
a soul
and a naked body.

*

   A single drop of water,
sexual seed
and thighs trembling in a park.

*

   Italic letters,
scattered stars,
a brown body full of ecstasy.

*

   Seventy years
passed;
the sound of grinding teeth.

*

   By your bedside
urine,
depression.

*

   By your bedside,
colors
don't reveal their secrets.

*

   Pull the trigger,
close your eyes and dream.
   White shines on the other side.

*

One after another,
sighs enter
the gate of emptiness.

*

Shut up, poet;
shut up,
poet.

*

Summer evenings;
ghosts compete
for water.

*

The tired man
stood there
to meditate.

*

On a lonely road,
my heart fluttered,
gazing at a wild rose.

*

A river hides
in a romantic
bubble.

*

Calculators in both hands,
and
nobody noticed.

*

The road they climbed
led to
a slaughterhouse.

*

Red, yellow, and white shoes
dream of
fresh almond blossoms.

*

The poet who crossed
the street couldn't
see the poem behind him.

*

Behind the road, white houses;
behind the white houses,
a sea and a sky.

*

The sun started to go down,
the sea sleeping
on the mountain's breast.

*

Night is getting darker,
butterflies fluttering
at the horizon.

*

In Tangier, dogs bark relentlessly
and farmers bend over
withered fields.

*

I have never been a storyteller,
I have never been
the wind's servant.

*

O guardian of the river,
don't wake
the sleepers on the beach.

*

The withered fields
listened and listened
and listened.

*

The tongue that
waited for the night to leave
has confessed.

*

Dim night
and dim day
fall into the mouth of time.

*

Behind the illuminated window,
a mother washes
her laughing child.

*

Midday:
behind a light pole,
a man in white clothes.

Qsaed Min AalaAlhadabaWaZilal Al-Raml

Poems from Above the Hill

1

Rain falls through the girl's hands onto the surface of the sea.
The trees, the hunter's dog waiting under the sand dunes,
and the gray clouds from the northwest
all watch the scene, breathing the reflection of light through the
fingers of the lovely girl.

Footsteps come quietly from behind the sand,
following the smell of rain,
while simple desires pass to the sea
as the cosmic music packs raindrops into the box of eternity.

2

His dreams slept in the muddy house;
his life's hopes rolled on an oak table.
He was a child practicing the new language;
red and yellow words raced him to the playground,
drawing squares and circles in the air,
clasping their edges like chairs that could take him to the sky.
It was a time that could fit easily into the hand.

3

Another evening goes to the edge of the valley.
The hunter will come tonight;
he'll pass his rough hands over her naked shoulders
and the shy robin will proclaim
the mysteries of the body's ecstasy.

4

Does the oak tree wail when its leaves fall?
asks the little bird walking behind its mother.
The twigs, crumbling to the ground, are terrifying;
the silence is terrifying,
and the arch on the horizon is far.

He'll reach it soon in the coming dawn,
says the mother, flying into the air.

5

Who is knocking on my door?
Who is playing under my window?
Who put the smell of peppermint in my backyard?
Who is climbing on my roof?
Who is staring at me with his magnificent eyes and not speaking?
Who has left the lovely, delicate laughter under my pillow, and
gone?
I can sleep now.

6

Footsteps of the lost can be heard close by,
but the heart is an echo of what the eye sees.
The earth touched his feet,
and those in back of him, gripped by cruel illusion
under a sky empty of everything except fear
are crying, but their voices don't rise.
Footsteps are not followed by footsteps,
but paths that curve towards distant dreams.

7

The morning
inside the cloak of wind
is a splendid morning.

8

Al-Aemma's bridge is moaning
from the weight of empty shoes,
from screams at the opening of the tunnel,
from breath rolled along by hateful feet,
from fire that burns the river grass.

Al-Aemma's bridge is a coffin
as large as

T
   H
      E
         C
            O
               U
                  N
                     T
                        R
                          Y

9

Through her window, she can see
the remote grain elevator white as ice.
Her thoughts go to the forest
where birds spread flickering passion and pure desire.
Electrical wires divide the gray space,
T.V. screens, dancing boys and girls,
old songs, newscasts, sadistic presidents,
soldiers waving their rifles before the masses,
and the scent of delicious cake.

10

The sea and I, silent—
we listen to the cosmos playing its instrument,
pouring out its favorite piece in B major.
The sea smiles at me;
I can't move for fear of damaging the music.

11

Time is so short: rapid footsteps on the wide asphalt—
where can I start my descent?
Here is a ladder offering itself
submissively in front of the National Judiciary Society.
From a high, colored signboard as wide as the street,
7-up bubbles sparkle,
and black cars traverse the town square.
Beside a colonnade of palm trees with dry empty fronds,
a traffic sign strictly follows the system.

Where can I start my descent to the abyss?

12

The scene repeats itself:
the café's glass door is open,
three wooden tables on the pavement,
a man wearing a khaki coat sits cross-legged,
leaning with his unshaven chin on his hand,
his eyes gazing at the heavy waitress who smells like cinnamon
while the morning walks quietly behind her…

The scene repeats itself…

The policeman, laughing, checking
the café's open glass door—

13

Oh, stories hide from the sleeper's eyes in tall grass;
I'll stand on guard,
the strokes of the clock will cover your laughter
and the warm rain will whisk the policeman away.

Oh,
the stories hide;
my fingers can't hold you,
the night can't prolong your dancing
and my pocket, unable to carry your children,
is full of runaway stories.

14

A river—between solid iron bars,
behind white, yellow and orange houses
near roaring trucks and magnificent cars,
parallel to men and women—
passes by;
some lean on shoulders, laughing;
some tremble with ecstasy;
some cry;
some piss;
and some die.

The same scene:
no need to stop;
a river sees everything;
the sources hold to the mouth of the river
where there's nobody.

15

In the early morning,
Café Al-Forsan
receives the sun with stately serenity;
the stairs are ready for innocent seduction
and a simple thought about life sits in the orange corner.

You alone cradle your coffee cup with an old man's wisdom.

16

With an autumn evening's tenderness,
the country girl leans on the city cornice;
from its house in the old seaport comes the sea,
holding the tranquility of the years in its palms.

Together, they dance in the martyrs' square.

17

I have to understand
the volcano's outrage
the devil's sibilance
the dance of fish in the water
the fire's hiss and the acrid smell of smoke
the trembling hands at the moment of touching
the laughter broken on cold beds

I have to understand
why eyes that didn't see life were closed

18

At the slope of the horizon, five lamps shine
and between the cement columns, one lamp by itself.
It isn't concerned with the birds asleep in their nests
nor with the man sitting at the computer
searching for words to use in a poem;
it isn't concerned with Beethoven

or with who wrote this sonata between 1796 and 1798
nor with Wilhelm Kempff who played it on December 12, 1951.
Nobody cares;
no one can know the depth of this eternal moment.

19

He leaves an elegant-looking bottle of milk in front of the door;
he doesn't feel thirsty
and has no desire to splash himself with cold water,
or to bring his nose close to the white carnation
to smell its fragrance with his eyes closed.
All he wants is to see sleep
sneaking quietly from the bedroom window.

20

There is a grand silence in this night's voices.
The last of the morning clouds look back as they approach;
the disk of the sun from behind the Moorish arch
scans the place sadly
and the mosque's muezzin reach Shahada with a broken voice.
The pigeons that landed on my roof all day
spread their wings and leave for the sky.
The moon lying on its orange bed watches from a distance.

21

Maybe it's the wind
Maybe it's the laughter of the guard in front of the T.V.
Maybe it's the coldness of midnight
Maybe it's the smell of the lonely gladiolus
Maybe it's the sparkling of her eyes at the hour of their meeting
Maybe it's the life that we don't know

22

Here I am crossing the street without fear,
I don't know how or why.
I feel proud that I crossed the street without fear.
Maybe it was not a real street.

23

In front of the house my brother stood
as he was lifted into the clouds that day.
The old shepherd waved his hand in the air,
following his sheep climbing the mountain.
We heard only a weak cry
as it lay on the doorstep.
He was cold in his gray robes,
like the winter that passed Qorina.

24

The wheat fields that witnessed our childhood
were smashed by crazy Gibli winds.
Rats, gerbils and turtles went to the mountaintop
while birds went to the sea.

Here comes the moon from behind the cedar tree with a pungent
shadow,
as if searching for something.

25

Yesterday, coming from the high stone village,
I remembered the time we spent near here in spring,
under the black stone,
where we met up with an armadillo.
We didn't know how it let us go toward the snail's hideaway.
I saw its eyes filled with fear
subtle as water.
I still carry a piece of that fear in my heart.

26

This morning, I was at the harbor
when the ships from Alexandria came;
Andronicus and his gang were there
counting slaves and wine barrels.
There was no mail in the ships,
and nobody knew anything about Hypatia.

27

Hypatia,
why are you sitting on the ruined porch?
The sun has arrived from behind the pomegranate tree
and the happy voices of young students
jump with the drops of water.
You sit silently in front of sleeping cat under the sun;
the sky hasn't left
nor is it in the grip of your small hand.
Do you understand the wind's words?
Or are you the morning itself, sitting in torment on the porch?

28

The streets of Alexandria are the gateway for strangers,
with their iron bars, their smoke like exhausted breath lashed by the
Gibli
and by their incomparable greed.
Those who came from the east were fascinated and buried in the
labyrinth;
those who came from the western desert
hid their eyes behind the veil of eternal solitude.

29

Hypatia,
do you hear the echo of morning's footsteps filled with the sea
breeze?
Do you hear the girl as she puts a rose on your doorstep?

That morning, the cardinal didn't get up so early,
it didn't care about prayer,
it had lost the desire to inspect the wide fields.
it was holding its heart,
listening to the crowds shouting in the streets of Alexandria
as your mutilated body washed toward the sea.

30

The evening is full of wind,
of cars entering the roads, children coming from school
swaying their little bodies
while pushing short words and laughter to the side of the road.
It doesn't matter what the wind will do;
it doesn't even matter if it runs away while we're sleeping before the dawn.
Really, it doesn't matter.
What matters is that I wake up in the morning
listening to the whisper of the grass under my window.

31

The road is narrow
but it ends at a marketplace and three walls.
The café waitress looks at the people with an accepting eye
while the gray cat licks a doll's finger under the chair.
Poster:
SPORTS REFRESH YOUR HEART
A GOOD DIET IS THE SECRET OF HEALTH
An archway, a door with a rusted handle;
the road is steep but it leads to the strangers' marketplace.

32

From far away, the ship's horn sounds feeble.
It's said that it belongs to tourists from France coming to the virgin land.
Parts of history that never belonged to them, were never theirs.
With open eyes behind digital cameras:
'…oh, how wonderful'
'…toasted pita'
'…eating with their hands'
'…the tall red hat is really sexy'
'…full of beauty'
'…what a magnificent creature'
'…why did the Romans leave this place?'

From far away comes a feeble voice of a weeping woman.
From a desert
…….
…….
a desert where nothing grows,
except fear.

33

I will be satisfied with just looking,
I won't open my mouth,
I will not listen to words, no matter how graciously they enter my ears.
The city is wrapped in darkness,
and heavy dreams escape from the sleeping tribes.

I will be satisfied with just looking,
I won't concentrate on the details of the city,
the city that embraced the fearful dawn in silence.

34

One—
Two—
Three—
The smell of fresh peppermint wafts up;
from the top of the stairs, her dress looks like a piece of the sky.
The wind moves softly.
The grape leaves hang over the entrance, surrendering gracefully.

One—
Two—
Three—
The dancing gypsy in her café
quietly welcomes the customers
on an evening released from a morning of grief.

35

Little ants run between my fingers;
I have no desire to follow them;
I have no desire to kill them.
Until this very moment, I do not understand
how they manage to seep quietly into the earth.
I lie on my back under the baryasania tree
and follow the fluttering of a bird's wings to the horizon.

36

The raindrops drip shyly on the beech tree.
The summer came and the winter left in a hurry,
didn't leave anything except raindrops
shyly
approaching
the beech tree.

37

As I was coming home in the evening
I didn't think of the thick clouds near the town square;
I didn't think of the moughrabia my neighbor is preparing for dinner.
I was just trying to remember a tune by Sami Alshawa,
an improvisation for the oud.

38

I try to write a poem
with my son Khalil
as we listen to James Taylor.
I ask him to start;
he smiles and says to me:
Let my brother Ali go first.
Don't write everything I say—
give it some thought.
Poetry needs ideas. Don't you think before you write?

He leans at the edge of the door
his hat in his hand, and gazes off,
searching for words for a poem.

39

The train has come exactly on time,
looking proud of its gray engine,
the large headlight and the sparkling wide orange line.
A street lamp bows with magnificent softness.
The two railway lines stretch out with ease.
The black leather bag stands behind the woman
who stands beside the man putting both hands in his pockets.
The train has come exactly on time,
proud of its engine.

40

Maybe I tend to be quiet because I'm a poet and so on,
but I didn't write for quite some time.
I tried, but the words—
they were rotting fruit,
moving objects in a forgotten alley.
Images: withered, trapped, compressed, neglected.
It is quite hard
to write a new poem.

41

Tonight, a meteor has fallen near the North Altwebia School.
Nobody was there;
the Moroccan had closed his shop
and the neighbors were watching:
I WILL NOT LIVE IN MY FATHER'S JELBAB.

42

People's voices melt like butter on the arch of forgetfulness.
The heart's curtain is wide open to the marketplace of the clouds.
A woman's arm rests on the café table that the sun can't reach;
her appointments are thrown on the pavement of wishes.

43

The bird can fly in the air as high as it desires
watching the trees covered by white snow,
the chickens running away to their muddy houses,
the children, their eyes illuminated behind closed windows.
The bird can listen to Charlie Parker playing,
the bird can dance with the raindrops without damaging a single song,
can dream about a place near the fireplace,
near the woman with the red dress
holding her soft hand and counting the beads of her necklace.

44

Who gave this dirt
the smell of fungus?
Who gave the volcano's heart the voices of old women?

Who hid such eloquence in this stony wall?

45

Sad drum beats come from a mountain empty of silence.
Quiver of dewdrops on the barren path
and fingers, rising high in the blankness,
line up with heavy rain and canals of Iranian crystal;
flowers bow to the stranger passing by.
Trees carry the night spaces in silence.

46

The traveler who raised his voice with the forbidden song
took my words and gave me his feet
to travel across the prairie of Candofan,
to hear the horses at the crossroads of desire.
The traveler who raised his voice with the forbidden song
took my food and gave me his hands
to hold the sacred flame.

47

Look straight out here;
the land shakes
with horses and thick dust.
Those who came with the evening and deceived the guards
laughed at the face of the sun resting on the horizon's arch.
They asked about birds that left their city one day
and asked about a millrace that had witnessed their weddings.
You held your hands to music at the side of the road
as the solitary dancer finished her dance,
and from his window, the child was counting fallen grapes with his fingers.
What do you hear in the book of voices but your heartbeat?

Look straight out here:
the pale land blanketed with serenity.

48

This is how the sea breeze comes:
laughing with happiness, it walks on the water
like a satisfied woman.
The sand bows to itself with a huge passion
and when immense breezes come, the voices
surrender to them with the great sea's silence.

49

Alone, an old man out on the sea,
with fish swimming at the sides of the old boat.
No fishing today;
is it the blue of the sky or the blue of the water?
You will be satisfied with a melody to give the master of the sea;
he knows you are tired
and that the fallen leaves cry without a sound.

50

In the night, when the hidden secrets emerge
and the neighbors' voices are hardly heard
and the bird sings its last song
nothing worries you
except the sounds of age, raining in the cold room.

51

Van Gogh enters the lobby, looking a little worried;
he scans the place with tired eyes
but sees only shadows
and the glass of water talking to sunlight near the small window,
the chair offering its back to the sleeping cat near fireplace,
and the pale yellow flowers clinging to the edge of the glass
as if they don't want to go.
Van Gogh exits the lobby, leaving his troubles on the high walls.

52

From his eastern window, Marcus Aurelius
watches Leda entering her oil bath.
She goes there early;
the servants massage her fragrant body,
their eyes sparkle as a winter's lightning dawn,
and the smell of rosemary fills the beach at Sabratha.
Aurelius is happy, he stretches his feet
on an Iranian silk with pictures of fighting buffalo;
he touches them gently so as not to bother Leda in her oil bath,
his joyful heart hears the yawning of the sea.

53

Wait for me at the crossroad,
says the girl waving her hand.
She doesn't say what day or time—
just *Wait for me*, waving her hand.
In the old café beside the tall oak tree
she sits, her large bag between her legs
facing the rising sun,
her jacket on the chair,
and between her fingers a flower she has saved from before.
Will he come? she wonders, following the march of ants on the oak tree.
He might have had another appointment.
She takes her bag, looking ahead to the road, and departs.

54

Creatures, you will go back to your homes,
I know it's time to listen;
the place doesn't worry itself with secrets,
and here the spring rises from the breast of the stone,
here the grass waves from afar to the women coming back from the fields,
here the Shepherd sings his favorite song into a gray space.

55

Sitting alone, watching cars of many colors pass the gray street—
the plain white, the metallic white, and the red.
You spot the neighbor's child behind the tree wearing his diaper;
the smell doesn't reach you.
Fifty cars have passed your square;
the child doesn't stop nor the old woman who smiles at you.
You can't bear the midday heat
but going back is a struggle.
The braids of Monet's girl have lost their color,
she smiles as if she were going to weep;
even the wine has left the glasses behind.

You will go back anyway,
you will open your ugly refrigerator,
you may find a bottle of Coca-Cola and insult America,
you may sleep on a bed with that smells like oxidized copper.
You are nothing but a lonely retired old man
with nothing but few years of insomnia and confused dreams
about an old cheap life.

56

The place can take this form in brown and gray,
something can start writing about copper.
It can say "…"
which ears can't hear.
A sound when it disappears
lingers as mere vibration on the wall,
on the roof, on the windows,
on the floor, on passersby as they look up.

57

Nothing is important there,
because the sky is high above us.
We can see only its blue dome,
hiding its stars in the light of a strong sun.
The wind doesn't concede to the domination of the sky,
it has what it wants,
between its own words and nobody's.
Today's wind is huge.
What else is there?
Yes, I see it, that dune behind the dry olive tree
You ask me, *What does it do?*
It grows.
Don't you know most things grow through their failures?
I do that.
You say you don't see the sea;
it is there between the folds of the land, laughing.

SAND SHADOWS

1

I know the blackness can't be fooled by the light of the window,
that a magnificent blue crowns your head,
that submissive eyes search for dreams far away,
and shoulders surrender to the relaxed gold silk;
lips keep many words locked away,
and an earring gracefully dangles from Allah's sky.
I know that you will leave with dignity and calm
as the ocean does when the eyes leave it alone.

2

Are those birds or caravans swimming through the air?
The blue won't speak about it,
and neither will those sitting on the bed in a warm room.

Are those houses a mirage of water or Bedouins hiding from old winds?
The sand won't speak about it
nor can foxes that stood on the hill for centuries follow their trails.

Are these the shadows of a city or a weeping flute?
The sound won't speak about it
and neither will dreams emerging from injustice.

3

The woman bends in her blue dress over white words;
light holds the carpet of space, feeling how the nearby edges
understand the thoughts
of the woman bending in her blue dress over white talk.
The eyes don't look over at the naked window,

and eyes don't watch the dance of the bee
over a yellow flower;
the eyes search the heart
of an eternal moment for white words.

4

Water finally reaches the pastry,
and the trembling hands sink in the light.
The lover doesn't come that night,
she doesn't light her lantern,
or open her box of secrets.
She doesn't lock her window,
but the pastry will soon be ready anyway.

5

In the garden of their passion,
the lovers sit, pouring wine
into jars of pleasure.
Two almond trees spread fragrant petals out to dry
on the greenery of the red garden;
a woman leans on her bed, satisfied as she approaches sleep,
and two white doves, glancing secretly,
follow the trembling of her naked breast.

6

The two girls who came before sunset to pick olives
knew that the one who traveled up to the high plateau
had imprinted secrets on the breast of the forest with his shocked
    finger;
the one who gathered animals in the wild lies on the wet grass
watching the alertness of horses in the space of time.
They knew what the cloud said when it passed the horizon in a flash
    of lightning

when thoughts come at a slant from a distant summer on city win-
dows
wiping the walls clear of what remains of sleepless nights.

7

Here I am
tracing a finger of desire
around the edges of a beautiful body,
turning over the tenants of the heart's secrets
and scattering silver.
Distant sand accompanies the birds
from a forest of worry,
stretching the tongues of words until their sighs
bless the face of the mountain-climber.
The walls stand in serenity while wise men watch
the two shadows dancing under a gray lantern.

8

The earth may borrow its blue
from passing clouds
or lay her fruit-laden body
as a banquet for wild animals.
In autumn evenings, it listens
to the ruckus of children at play,
debating with the stubborn horizon
about the virginity of dawn.
It sleeps like a saint forgetting
how to pronounce words,
but has never kept company with the house
standing there on the high hill,
guarding it from the eastern sky.

9

Water doesn't turn back to the houses
standing in sunlight;
water carries its wooden boats
to a cave of a dark lake.
Across the horizon, it spreads
a feast for enchanting nymphs
and in eternity, collides
with the curve of the earth.

10

The distant echoes are clear and high
like trees in the wind
fluttering with planets in a faraway sky,
taking softness and ripples and an image
of water to the ground of the heart
where everything is allowed.
Distant echoes stand in a courtyard
collecting dreams of a lover,
staring at the sunlight
and hanging a magnificent song
at the fork of the road.
The distant echoes don't look back;
they follow the silk of whispers
and walk silently to the graves.

11

Who tied that horse to a black wooden pole?
His two front legs strike the ground.
Who asked for help from horses of faraway villages?
This horse shakes the rope with great force;
he thinks about the wind that betrayed him
in the desert that has forgotten him.

The horse does not think of the black wooden pole;
he doesn't see it.

12

A knight, a bow, an arrow and a black horse
cross the desert in silence.
The horse doesn't ask his master
about doves flying in the distance,
doesn't ask about a fox trapping a small hedgehog
under the dry acacia tree,
doesn't ask about the hills of sand that do not cling to pebbles,
or about the whistling winds near high hills;
he doesn't ask about his longing
for the gray mare of his dark childhood.
He just listens to his own mumbling
with a lot of sadness.

13

A writer sits in the oak grove;
the wind doesn't come into his garden this evening.
He doesn't turn to look at the dancing tree near the fence,
and he doesn't turn to look at the girl lighting the incense.
The writer is sad this evening
because words no longer belong to him
and because images he played with have run wildly away.
Sitting in an oak grove, what does a writer do
but look at his trembling hand.

14

The window has turned its back on the blue sky;
it is distracted by the dancers who have entered the room,
by the girl whose long hair caresses her full breasts,
by the walls moving shadows of desire in front of her eyes.

The window is happy with the bodies that surround it in ecstasy;
"The sky will have another day,"
says the window in a whisper.

15

Then there's a moment
when rocks that clung to the mountaintop
swim in a thin haze.
Now they can feel the water's body,
can see people from a new angle.
How close they are to the green grass
and to palm trees waving and smiling.
Rocks don't have to look down now,
don't have to fight the clouds every morning.
The rocks must look up
and dive as deeply as possible into water.

16

What remains of the woman standing in front of the mirror
if we cast a veil over the light from the open door?
Heavy shadows on the mirror's surface.
What remains of the woman standing in front of the mirror
if she didn't turn towards the white flowers?
A sad flute plays on the mirror's surface.
What remains of the woman standing in front of the mirror
if she didn't stand in front of the mirror?
A poem waiting on the mirror's surface.

17

In the upper half of the carpet,
in a green circle, a man and a woman--
maybe they're arguing
or maybe they're about to embrace.

Maybe they'll separate
but they're not going anywhere.

On both sides of the green circle,
red sugar cane and two doves:
maybe they're from the Gulf of Arabia;
or maybe they're relics from Andalusia.

The red sugar cane doesn't swing
and the two doves don't fly off.
Low inside the green circle,
there are triangles and circles;
sighs float up as large as a palm.

In front of the carpet, men stand
in a jellabiya of Marrakech wool
watching and watching, in their turbans from Fez.
Maybe they are talking all day;
maybe they are talking all night.

18

The silver ring encircles a delicate finger,
saying what isn't declared
by the thick henna on the back of the hand.
The tattoo emerges from a corner
of the forehead to sleepy pink flowers
in the palm of the hand.
It is not bothered by the shine of the silver;
it is not bothered by the Berber carvings,
or by the narrow stone window
or by the shower of hesitant light
on the Berber girl's shoulders.

19

The master of the house is pleased to sit
like a respected lord on his throne, giving orders.
In his long hat, the head of security
assumes his role in a royal place —
he shakes his head and slaps his thigh
so the audience can see.

Because the oud player has a long dress,
she can open her legs in the royal room
while improvising in B minor.
She moves her fingers across the strings.
She doesn't know that her daughter spit blood this morning,
that her husband can't sleep and recites his rosary.

In the royal place,
everything is within the master's reach;
the head of security moves his head
and slaps his thigh so the audience can see.
In the royal room the child dies,
and the husband chokes on his rosary.

20

Let's enter the poet's room:
four paintings above the bed,
a wooden chair near the table,
the window that stopped the night from entering looks at him,
a rectangular mirror traps the lantern's light,
an extra chair near the door for the poet's girlfriend,
over the table,
a bottle of water,
papers,
a pencil,
and a glass of wine.
Let's leave the poet's room
and let the poems grow until the morning.

21

At night,
at a specific hour in the night,
on the east side of the city,
near the bridge,
a cloud spreads its blue head-scarf on sleeping houses.
Tell the lanterns waiting on the bridge
to dip into the water;
let the moon sit on a high rock
and put its bright fish into the water.
Call each one by name,
And look up to the unlit houses.
You can catch the sighing through the cracks of the doors.

22

The sailor sat in the corner
where the light of the cheap tavern did not steal his shadow.
He was thinking of the forest at the head of the mountain--
was he supposed to go over there?
Was that where the woman he dreamed of was waiting?
She called to him, softly stroking his beard:
You won't ever take the ocean,
it will take you to the edge of time and will leave you alone;
the mat on the ocean floor is short
and its fire-sticks are thin;
you drink the juice of grapes from places you can't remember
as the ocean drinks from your lost eyes
and the flame of your life disappears.

23

The boats that returned to the shore lowered their sails and said
    nothing.
Other boats had lost their sails months ago,
their masts knocked down by the hand of winds.

Holding its head high, the shore said:
Where are the bronze men that entered the sea?
Where are the spices that cast their fragrance to the wind?
Where are the slaves and whistles? Where are the clams and red
    shells?
The boats returning to shore lowered their sails,
sighed deeply and looked to the sea that took the tide
to islands on the horizon.

24

In autumn, the village likes to dress its houses in crimson.
The dreams of those returning from the fields,
lying down after drinking tea,
are also crimson.
Men and women are joined together,
while insects make sexual noises –
the sperm is crimson,
the egg is crimson.

25

The village has seven doors
one for winter
one for spring
one for summer
one for autumn
one for wide space
one for silent earth
and one for the poem.

26

Then the stranger entered the village with the morning,
followed by a bird that had perched on a wooden fence,
tucking its song into its wings.

The white clouds raised their necks over the oak trees
and said
Who is walking near the high reef?
Could it be the soldier taken by the war,
or the one from the valley kidnapped by wolves?

The stranger that entered the village with morning
left before the dreams of the village awoke.

27

A sea spouts from the side of the woman sleeping on the snow,
carrying masculine seeds of proud mountains;
the water neighs like horses galloping on the wings of the wind
embracing along the way
the voices of clay and the luggage of departing ones.
The sea
its beginning
prayer
the end
prayer
the surface of the sea
my skin
its waves
my churning worries
its path
my anchor tossed out to the universe
its fish
my fingers
I dipped in the water
its flow
my eye
lights the ocean
so it won't fall into the abyss

28

For the singer:
a relief when the tune carries him to yellow sand.
For the naked man:
keys of his anxiousness as he stands in front of his heaven
looking to the ground repeating the creation of the alphabet.
For the naked woman:
a purity of soul as she resting her child against the hand of amaze-
ment.
For those coming from everywhere:
wagons of desire carrying their hearts to new shores.
For those leaving without belongings:
judgment of light lifting them to the calm of eternity.
For the prayers:
doors.
For the prayers:
doors
hanging on beds of time.

29

A green fish dangles from an eagle's talons,
the spines of a cactus are in a man's neck at the end of the line,
they can't steal a glimpse of the girl's body standing near the river
nor can the bird return the melody that fell on her breasts;
proud crimson enters the woman's calm fingers,
and fire hides in the shadows of the garden.

30

In the morning,
the children sit in their mothers' laps
waiting for fishermen;
night arrives alone in the ship of the moon
and those that left were taken by the sun
to new shores.

The sails have become flags
swaying with weeping women
in lost winds.

31

Marcus Aurelius passed by here;
he stood in front of the marble arch
noticing the carvings stealing the sound of the sea,
there wasn't a strand of grass or a twig
or a grain of sand or a drop of rain,
the soldiers were covered in armor and weaponry
lined up around the marble arch,
and the woman were dancing to the Bedouin music.
The weeping behind them was greater than the emperor;
he wasn't aware of what the wind was doing
in the village square without grass or twigs.

New Poems

WHAT DIRECTION

The windows of your heart face
a courtyard of absurdity;
in what direction
does the face of questions turn?

When your people watered their voices,
you spoke.
When you threw what you threw,
the gazelle ran crying,
and you returned.

When you cushioned your head from your only dream,
you swallowed a star in a faraway sky;
when you clenched your fist,
the night leaked its whiteness.

In what direction
do you turn the face of questions?

FEAR

I'm afraid to pour words on the surface
of the past.
I'm afraid to dive into the central shyness
of the waves.
I fear the softness of sleeping pebbles
on the sand.
I fear entering a dream in the crack
of darkness.
I fear the rain is falling into the bowl of humanity's
nonexistence.
I fear windows opening
on things.
I'm afraid that shadows without bodies populate
countries.
I'm afraid that fear is empty
of meaning.

CLOUDS

The men clouds.
The women clouds.
The baby clouds, the sheik clouds, the elderly people clouds.
Circular clouds, tunnel clouds.
Tree clouds, birds, elephants, ducks and lions.
The ant clouds, the teacups, the elevators, the stations.
. . . .
. . . .
The clouds rise to the mountain of the sky,
to an oasis or lake or forest or courtyard.

THE ROCK

The one who rose before dawn saw what happens on the rock:
this is the road to wilderness, and from here, the river horses go to
    the crow.
He drew back his arrow towards the fire wagon
and anointed the hoof prints of his horse with henna,
saying to the beautiful women:
Wander and gather what falls from light;
make a symbol from the guardian ibex of the mountain.
And to the brown ox:
Why do you bow your head when the hunters are gone?
Is it the sins of the mountain barmaid, or is that a scent that races
    from over there?"
He said:
the white of the rock is the inner monster withdrawn in shadows.

THE FINGER OF THE HAND

With my little finger,
I open and close my eye
caught up in the confusion of colors—
all the colors.
I enter the kingdom of shapes:
a man with one leg and a walking stick above his head,
two pigeons and a monkey under a tree—he seems to be sleeping—,
dangerous aircraft for war,
a big water bowl and dancing fish,
forests and fires and bats and ladders,
a dome, and bushels of dates, and crows, and horses,
a watch tower, and fountains, and gold flasks, and wagons and—
with the movement of a finger, everything disappears.

A GLIMPSE OF FAYOUM

One distant morning,
the Nile hid the whispers of a woman who had tied her story with
    string
to the back of a calf with golden horns,
nothing was there except a skylark picking at slender grains of
    wheat;
the king's caravan wasn't there to place his belongings on the high
    hill,
and the water bearers didn't return from the cave of eternal thirst.
Silent men turned pages of the soil;
secretly they read the names of her family.
The mother scattered her tears over mourners,
and fountains of blood trickled over the hennaed fingernails.
The girl going to sleep – who gave her silver earrings?
Who outlined the eyebrows in dark black?
Who gave the cheeks a blush of fresh apples?
Who straightened her hair with a hand of pleasure?
Who found comfort in those two wide eyes?
As she brought her lips close to him, the river could only hear cov-
    ered whispers.
How could he have acted any differently?

DESIRE AND OTHER THINGS

Tender desire is hung:
between air and foam,
between the actor and the watcher,
between a fluttering breast and a relenting night,
between the arrival of sighs and their departure,
between slow and hasty suspicions ,
between enduring cries and indecent laughter.

Tender erotic desire
creeps towards the edge of trembling
almost
......
......
dying.

KNOWLEDGE

I don't know how to count on my fingers,
but I can distinguish sounds in deserts.
I can't pronounce letters and words,
but I can guard the river with gestures.
I don't know how to walk in gardens,
but I can listen to insects.
I don't know how to sleep in the moonlight,
but I can embrace darkness until it yields its secrets.

Acknowledgments

Ashur Etwebi writes: "I would like to thank Brenda Hillman who gave tremendous effort and patience for this book to come to light. Brenda Hillman worked on the translation with Diallah Haidar, whom I would like to thank deeply for all the time and effort that she gave. My thanks also go Jon Thompson, who was enthusiastic about this project. Many thanks to Jillian Kurvers for typing the manuscript. Thanks, too, to the online journals *words without borders*, and *Free Verse*."

About the Author

Ashur Etwebi, lives in Tripoli, Libya. A poet, novelist, and translator, he has published six books of poetry, two novels, and three books of translation.

About the Translators

Brenda Hillman is the author of eight collections of poetry, the most recent of which is *Practical Water*. She is the Olivia C. Filippi Professor of Poetry at Saint Mary's College in Moraga, California.

Diallah Haidar is a Lebanese-American and a native speaker of Arabic. She graduated from the University of California Berkeley with a BA degree in English Literature and in Near Eastern Studies. She received her MA degree from Columbia University in Middle Eastern, South Asian, and African Studies.

Free Verse Editions

Edited by Jon Thompson

13 ways of happily by Emily Carr
A Map of Faring by Peter Riley
An Unchanging Blue: Selected Poems 1962-1975 by Rolf Dieter Brinkmann, translated by Mark Terrill
Between the Twilight and the Sky by Jennie Neighbors
Blood Orbits by Ger Killeen
Child in the Road by Cindy Savett
Current by Lisa Fishman
Divination Machine by F. Daniel Rzicznek
Physis by Nicolas Pesque, translated by Cole Swensen
Poems from above the Hill & Selected Work by Ashur Etwebi, translated by Brenda Hillman and Diallah Haidar
Puppet Wardrobe by Daniel Tiffany
Quarry by Carolyn Guinzio
remanence by Boyer Rickel
Signs Following by Ger Killeen
The Flying House by Dawn-Michelle Baude
The Prison Poems by Miguel Hernández, translated by Michael Smith
The Wash by Adam Clay
These Beautiful Limits by Thomas Lisk
Under the Quick by Molly Bendall
Verge by Morgan Lucas Schuldt
What Stillness Illuminated by Yermiyahu Ahron Taub
Winter Journey [Viaggio d'inverno] by Attilio Bertolucci, translated by Nicholas Benson